Drumset

DAVE BLACK

SANDY FELDSTEIN

Alfred's MAX™ is the next best thing to having your own private teacher. No confusion, no frustration, no guesswork—just lessons that are well paced and easy to follow. You listen to the music you're learning to play and watch a professional show how it's done, then get time to stretch out and put it all together. No matter how you like to learn, Alfred's MAX™ series gives you the ultimate learning experience at a screamin' deal of a price.

Cover drumset photos courtesy of Yamaha Corporation of America. Photos on pages 5 and 6, the bottom row of page 7 and at bottom-right of page 8 by Karen Miller.

Copyright © MMIV by Alfred Publishing Co., Inc.
All rights reserved. Printed in USA.
ISBN 0-7390-3466-9 (Book and DVD)

CONTENTS

About the DVD

The DVD contains valuable demonstrations of all the instructional material in the book. You will get the best results by following along with your book as you watch these video segments. Musical examples that are not performed with video are included as audio tracks on the DVD for listening and playing along.

INTRODUCTION

Alfred's MAX™ Drumset is an innovative and practical approach to learning to play drums. You'll play an actual beat in your first lesson and quickly incorporate techniques for hi-hat, ride cymbal, snare drum and bass drum. The two performance sections of the book, "Playing Rock" and "Playing Jazz," provide more interesting and useful practice material than most other methods, with beats and fills designed to work well and be used in performance situations.

The DVD contains valuable demonstrations of all the instructional material in the book, providing many of the same benefits you would gain from lessons with a live instructor. By watching these video segments as you listen to the performance and follow along with the book, you'll learn to play with correct form and motion and quickly develop the ability to read music notation. Audio tracks of the three drum charts and all beats and fills are also included on the DVD for listening and playing along.

As with any method, the best results are achieved with daily practice. Set aside a reasonable amount of time each day—at least 30 minutes. Some lessons will require more time.

We hope you enjoy this book and DVD and congratulate you in your pursuit of musical excellence.

The Authors

ARRANGING YOUR DRUMSET

The Overall Setup

Arrange your drums and cymbals around you in a way that will minimize reaching, stretching and twisting. The drums should be set up to accommodate you—not the reverse. Note that instructions regarding left-to-right placement of drums, etc., will be reversed for left-handed players.

The Throne

Proper positioning of the throne is very important as it affects both balance and the ability to use your feet effectively. The throne's distance from the drums affects reach, while its height affects foot movement. You must experiment with both factors until optimum placement is achieved.

The Snare Drum

The standard snare drum is 14 inches in diameter. Whether you play with matched or traditional grip (see page 6), position and angle the snare drum so that the proper alignment of your forearms and hands is not adversely affected. With matched grip, the snare drum is usually flat or slanted slightly downward toward the player; with traditional grip, the snare drum is usually tilted slightly downward toward the right (if the player is right-handed).

The Bass Drum

The bass drum, also referred to as the *kick drum,* may have one or two heads. It is usually between 18 and 26 inches in diameter, but the most common size is 22 inches. It is played with a beater operated by a foot pedal. The bass drum beater may be made of hard felt, plastic or wood. A second bass drum may be added to the basic five-piece setup. Using a rug or mat is strongly recommended as it protects the floor and the bottom of the drum and keeps the drum from sliding forward as it is played.

The Mounted (Rack) Tom-Toms

Drummers may use one or more mounted toms ranging in size from 10 to 15 inches in diameter. When using more than one tom, position them so there are no large gaps in height between batter heads or between the drums. When attaching the toms to the mount on top of the bass drum, be sure they don't touch or rub against the bass drum, snare drum, or floor tom. Tilt the toms slightly toward you so that the drumstick clears the rims when striking the heads. Avoid a severe drumstick angle to produce the best tone and reduce the likelihood of damaging the drumhead.

The Floor Tom-Tom

The size of the floor tom-tom is usually within a range of 14 to 16 inches in diameter. Position the floor tom at approximately the same height as the snare drum. You may angle the drum slightly towards you or the snare drum.

The Hi-Hat

The hi-hat consists of a pair of 14- to 15-inch cymbals that are mounted "facing" one above the other. A foot pedal is operated that brings the cymbals together to produce a crisp "chick" sound. The most popular combination of hi-hat cymbals is a medium-thin top cymbal and a medium or medium-heavy bottom cymbal. Place the hi-hat to the left of (and slightly higher than) the snare drum.

The Ride Cymbal

The ride cymbal is usually 19 to 22 inches in diameter and of medium to medium-heavy weight. It should be mounted on a cymbal stand that includes felt washers and a piece of rubber tubing that serve as a cushion between the stand and the cymbal. The wing nut should never touch the cymbal because it will restrict the cymbal's sound and can also cause it to crack. Position the ride cymbal so that the stick is able to strike it two to four inches from the edge.

The Crash Cymbals

Drummers use one or more crash cymbals ranging from 16 to 18 inches in diameter and of thin to medium weight. Position your crash cymbals within normal reach and tilt them slightly so the shaft of the drumstick will strike the edge. Some drummers place their cymbals above normal playing range to maximize the visual effect.

BASIC SETUP

GETTING STARTED
Holding the Sticks

Holding the drumsticks in the correct manner and position is very important to developing proper technique, attack and control. There are two primary ways of holding the drumsticks: the *matched grip* and the *traditional grip*. We will use the matched grip throughout this volume.

MATCHED GRIP

When using the matched grip, each hand holds the drumstick in the same manner. Think of the stick as a natural extension of your arm as you follow these steps to form the matched grip:

1. Grip the stick one-third of the way from the butt end with your thumb and the first joint of your index finger.

2. Close the other fingers loosely around the stick; they will be used to help control its movement.

3. Turn your hand so that the back faces upward when playing. The stick should be in line with the wrist and arm.

Figure 4 is a view of both hands using matched grip.

Fig. 1

Fig. 2

Fig. 3

Fig. 4

TRADITIONAL GRIP

When using the traditional grip, the right-hand hold is the same as for matched grip. The correct grip for the left hand is formed as follows:

1. Place the stick in the socket between your thumb and index finger so that one-third of the stick at the butt-end extends behind your hand. The grip should be just tight enough to cause a slight drag if you were to try to pull the stick from your hand (fig. 5).

2. Allow the first two fingers to rest lightly on top of the stick (the first more lightly than the second) to act as a guide (fig. 6). Rest the stick across the third finger, which will act as a support. The fourth finger should rest against the third finger (fig. 7).

Fig. 5

Figure 8 is a view of both hands using traditional grip.

Fig. 6

Fig. 7

Fig. 8

The Snare Drum Stroke (also used for Tom-Toms)

Sound is produced by striking the top head of the snare drum to set the air inside the drum in motion, causing the bottom head and the snares to vibrate. When striking any drumhead, the best sound is achieved when the sticks are allowed to rebound from the head as quickly as possible.

The *stroke* is produced using a down-up motion of the wrist:

Fig. 9

1. Place the tip of the stick on the head (figs. 9 & 10).

2. From the wrist, raise the tip of the stick as far from the head as possible.

Fig. 10

Fig. 11

3. Execute the stroke by striking the head and immediately returning to the up position (figs. 11 & 12).

When alternating strokes, the right stick strikes the drum and rebounds to a position approximately two inches above the head. When the left stick comes down, the right stick goes from the low position to the full up position.

Fig. 12

Playing the Bass Drum

There are two basic techniques for playing the bass drum:

1. When using the *heel down* technique, the entire foot contacts the pedal. To execute the stroke, rock your foot to make the beater strike the head, then immediately return your foot to the up position (figs. 13 & 14).

2. When using the *heel up* technique, the heel is raised off the pedal surface while the ball of the foot operates the pedal. Immediately return your foot to the up position after the head is struck (figs. 15 & 16).

Fig. 13   Fig. 14   Fig. 15   Fig. 16

Bass Drum Pedal Tension Adjustment

Adjust the pedal's spring tension so that the beater does not touch the head when your foot rests on the pedal. The tighter the pedal tension, the faster and stronger the rebound. Remember that the beater should not remain against the head after impact. The rebound principle described for the snare drum stroke applies to all drums.

Playing the Hi-Hat

The hi-hat is operated with your left foot. When at rest, the space between the cymbals should be approximately one to two inches; when the foot pedal is pressed, the cymbals come together. You can also strike the top hi-hat cymbal with the tip of a drumstick while the cymbals are closed, partially open, or completely open. A good "chick" sound can be produced by slightly tilting the bottom cymbal.

I to 2 inches

There are two basic techniques for playing the hi-hat with the foot:

1. The *heel-toe* or *rocking* technique is often used when playing on beats 2 and 4. In this case, as the ball of the foot presses the pedal down, the heel rises off the pedal, and when the heel goes down, the ball of the foot rises (fig. 17).

2. The *toe* technique is great when playing rapid rhythms. Here, the leg is raised to keep the heel off the pedal while the ball of the foot bounces up and down to activate the cymbals (fig. 18).

Hi-Hat Pedal Tension Adjustment

Tension the hi-hat spring so there is strong resistance when you place your foot on the pedal. The tighter the pedal tension, the faster and stronger the rebound.

Fig. 17

Fig. 18

Striking the Ride Cymbal

The ride cymbal has a number of playing areas, and each area produces a different sound. Striking the ride cymbal near the bell produces a high-pitched "ping" sound (very effective for Latin-American rhythms and funk). Striking near the edge produces a broader sound. The best area for playing the ride-cymbal rhythm is about one-third of the way in from the edge (fig. 19).

You can create other interesting effects by using the tip, shoulder, or butt end of the drumstick to play the ride cymbal.

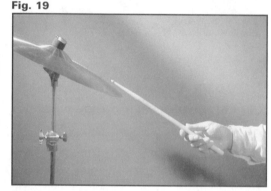

Fig. 19

It is very important to balance the volume between the ride cymbal, hi-hat cymbals, bass drum and snare drum. Listen carefully to the blending of all sounds.

MUSIC NOTATION

Measures

Music notes are shown on a group of lines and spaces called a *staff,* which is divided into equal parts called *measures.*

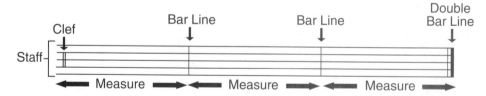

Clef | Bar Line | Bar Line | Double Bar Line
Staff
Measure — Measure — Measure

Bar lines indicate where measures begin and end.

A *double bar line* has one thin line and one thick line, and appears at the end of a piece.

At the beginning of each line of music, there is a *clef sign*. Unpitched percussion music uses the neutral clef (‖).

A *repeat sign* has two dots before a double bar line (:‖) and means to go back to the opposite-facing repeat sign (‖:) and play the music again. If there is no such additional sign, then repeat from the beginning of the music.

Notes & Rests

The duration of musical sounds (how long or short they are) is indicated by using different types of notes. Corresponding symbols called *rests* are used to indicate equivalent durations of silence.

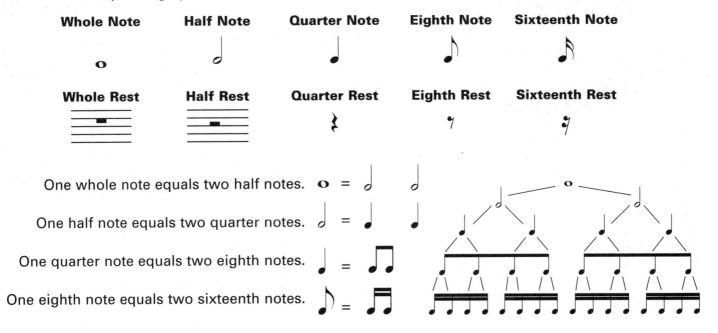

One whole note equals two half notes.
One half note equals two quarter notes.
One quarter note equals two eighth notes.
One eighth note equals two sixteenth notes.

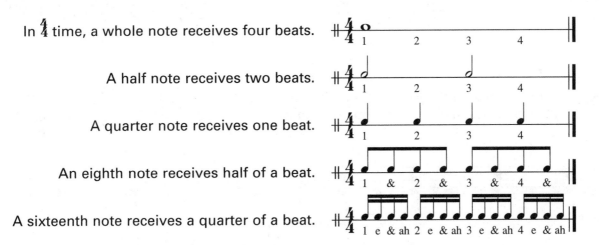

The Time Signature

A *time signature*, a symbol with two numbers, is placed at the beginning of a piece of music to indicate how the music is counted:

4 The top number shows the number of *beats* (or *counts*) in each measure, in this case, four.
4 The bottom number shows what kind of note gets one beat, in this case, a quarter note (♩).

In 4/4 time, a whole note receives four beats.

A half note receives two beats.

A quarter note receives one beat.

An eighth note receives half of a beat.

A sixteenth note receives a quarter of a beat.

Tempo

Tempo is the speed of a musical piece or passage. Tempo is indicated by a musical term or by an exact *metronome marking*. A *metronome* is a device that clicks or flashes lights to indicate the tempo. For example, ♩ = 120 means the metronome will click 120 times per minute, and each click represents a quarter note.

Drum Notation

Each line and space of the staff designates a particular drum or cymbal.

PLAYING ROCK

Basic Rock Beats

Play the following basic beat in which the right hand (R.H.) on the ride cymbal and the right foot (R.F.) on the bass drum play together.

In many beats, the left hand (snare drum) and the left foot (hi-hat) play together as in the next example.

Here's a basic beat that combines the hands and feet. All of the following examples can also be played with the bass drum only on beats 1 and 3.

Often, the right stick is used to play the hi-hat, which may be partially closed (cymbals lightly touching) or tightly closed. In such cases, the left foot applies light or heavy pressure on the hi-hat pedal.

By changing the right-hand quarter notes to eighth notes, we create a more interesting beat. Example 5 uses the right hand on the ride cymbal. In example 6, the right hand moves to the hi-hat.

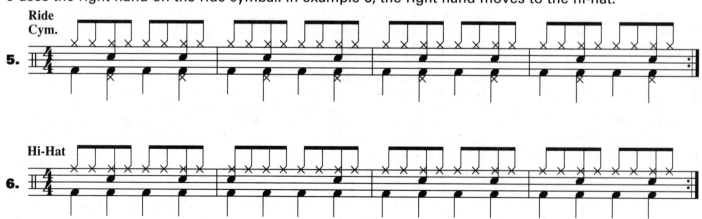

Embellishing the Left Hand

Eighth notes can also be played by the left hand. Practice all of these beats first with the right hand on the ride cymbal and then on the hi-hat.

The left hand is used to play other drums as well. Example 4 adds the mounted tom-tom; examples 5 and 6 add the floor tom-tom, while example 7 incorporates both tom-toms.

Embellishing the Bass Drum

So far, the bass drum has played quarter notes on all four beats. Now, we'll change that rhythm somewhat.

After practicing these examples with the right hand on the hi-hat, repeat them with the right hand on the ride cymbal. When playing the right hand on the ride cymbal, add the hi-hat on beats 2 and 4.

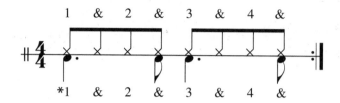

*A dot (·) placed after a note increases its value by one half the value of the original note.

Any of the previous beats can be used with these three bass drum patterns.
We suggest you repeat each rhythm four to eight times.

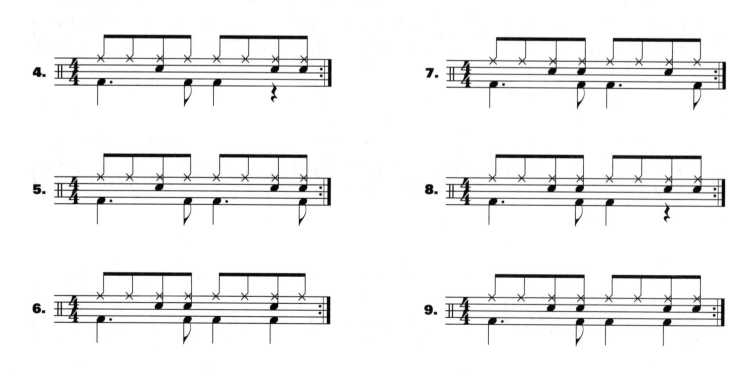

Embellishing the Left Hand and Bass Drum

The dotted-quarter eighth-note bass drum patterns can also be used with beats where the left hand moves around the drumset. Practice the examples in order horizontally across the page as well as vertically. Repeat each pattern four to eight times.

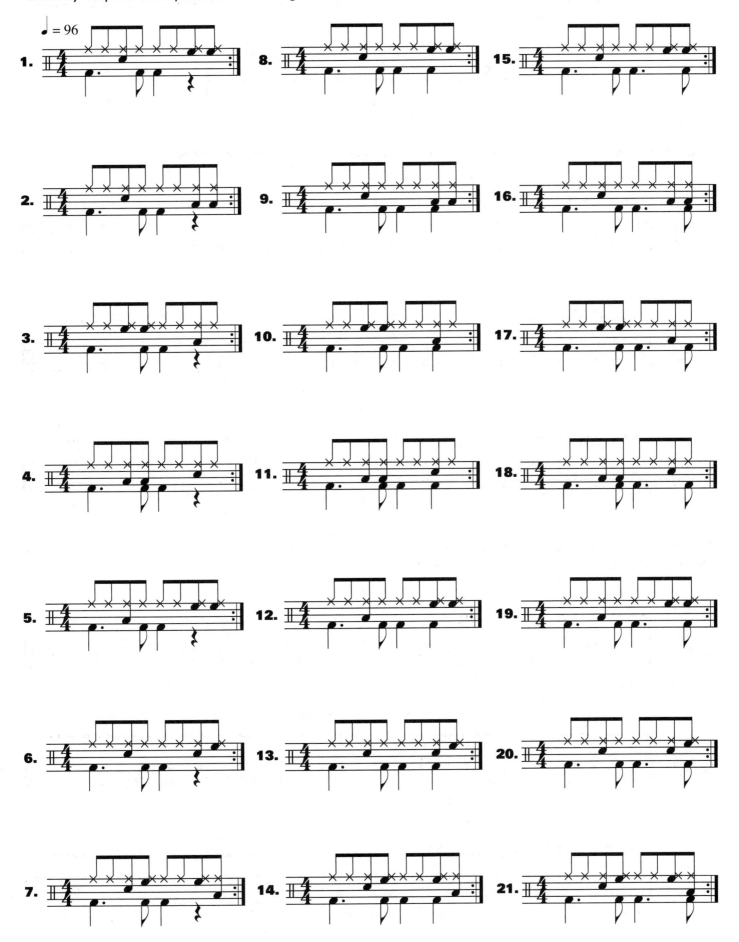

More Advanced Bass Drum Beats

Very often, the right and left hands remain constant while the bass drum becomes busier. Once you've mastered these beats, you may use your left hand on other drums as shown on the preceding page. Repeat each pattern four to eight times.

Rock Drum Fills in Context

Drum fills are usually played at the ends of musical phrases, serving as bridges that connect ideas. Always practice fills in a musical "time" setting, playing three bars of time followed by the one-bar fill.

Example:
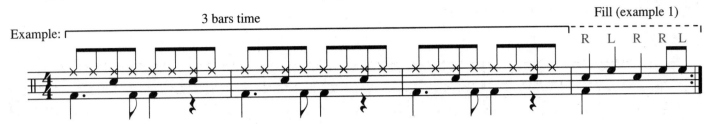

You may use any of the beats in the previous exercises for the time pattern. Play this page as a complete study, moving from fill to fill, in any order, without stopping. Remember to always play three bars of time between fills. Although fills break away from the basic beat, they should not speed up or slow down.

1.

2.

3.

4.

5.

6.
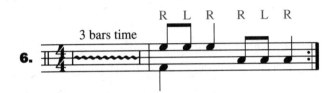

7.

8.

9.

10.

More Fills

Try playing the first note of each bar on the ride cymbal to create an interesting variation. This technique is demonstrated in the following patterns, but you should experiment with more of your own. Play three bars of time before each fill.

The fills in the next group are based on sticking patterns known in rudimental-style snare drumming as the *paradiddle-diddle* and *double paradiddle*.

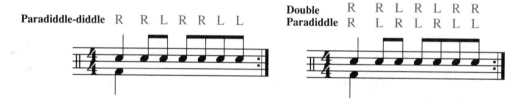

Play three bars of time before each fill. Practice the examples in order horizontally across the page as well as vertically.

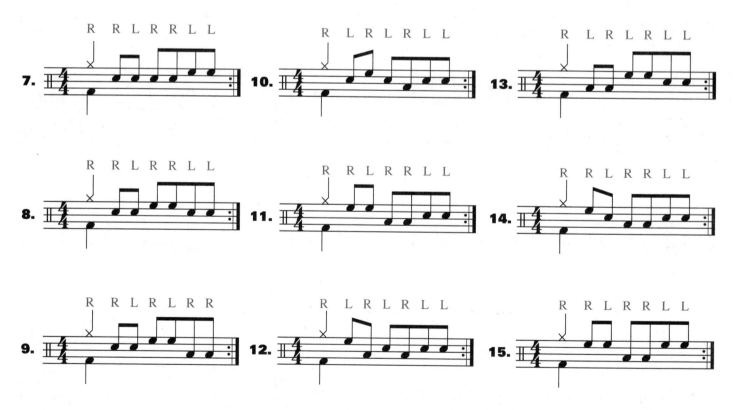

Two-Bar Rock Fills

In this section, you'll play two bars of time followed by a two-bar drum fill. You may use any of the patterns from the previous exercises. Play this page as a complete study, moving from fill to fill in any order without stopping. Always remember to play two bars of time between fills.

*The *flam* is a combination of a small note (called a *grace note*) and a main note, used to produce a *tenuto* (a broader sound). The sticks don't strike the head at the same time, but close enough to sound almost like a single stroke. If the grace note is played by the left hand, the main note is played by the right, and vice versa.

** > = *Accent*. Play the note a little louder.

BLUES FOR TIME

The blues is based on a 12-bar form made up of three 4-bar phrases. Many tunes require a fill only in the twelfth bar, but sometimes the music requires fills in bars four and eight as well. After playing the tune as written, try using any of the previous beats and fills you've learned.

Blues for Time is presented twice on the DVD, first with drums, then without drums so you can play along.

COMPOSED AND ARRANGED
BY GORDON BRISKER

*
$\boxed{\%}$ = repeat the previous bar.

Sixteenth-Note Fills

Practice these fills in order horizontally across the page as well as vertically.

♩ = 96

1.

7.

2.

8.

3.

9.

4.

10.

5.

11.

6.

12.

More Advanced Bass Drum Beats

Adding dotted-eighth sixteenth-note patterns to the bass drum creates some interesting variations.

Embellishing the Left Hand

You can also add sixteenth notes to the snare drum and ride cymbal/hi-hat.
The bass drum pattern is constant in examples 1–3 and 4–7.

Embellishing the Hands and Feet

Two-Bar Fills Using Sixteenth Notes

In this section, you will play two bars of time followed by a two-bar drum fill. As in the previous section, you may use any of the previous beats and should play the page as a complete study, moving from fill to fill without stopping. Remember that although fills break away from the basic beat, they should not speed up or slow down.

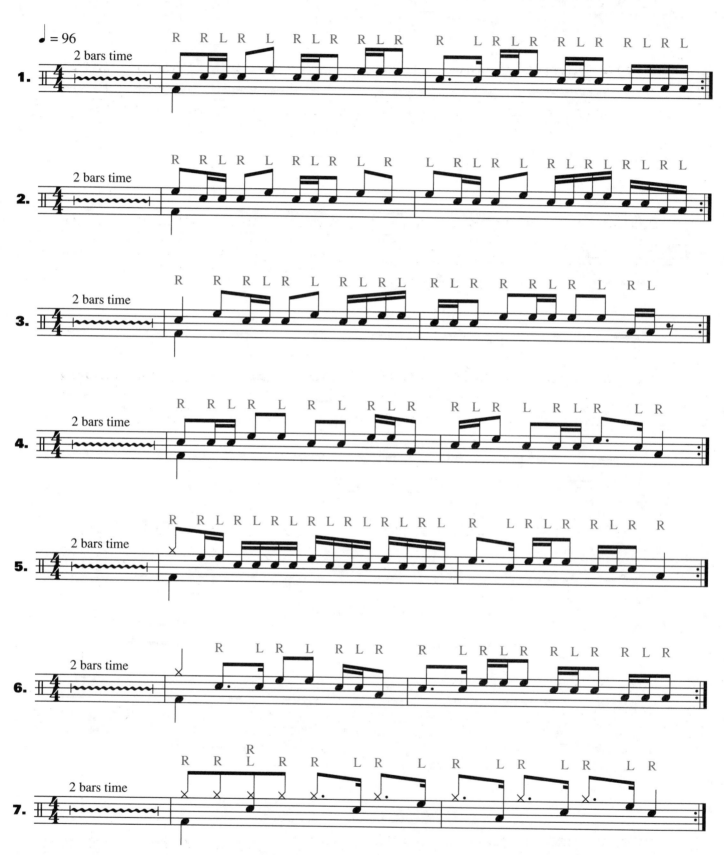

Before continuing further, go back to the chart of *Blues for Time* on page 18 and play it using beats and fills that incorporate sixteenth notes.

Sixteenth Notes on the Hi-Hat

Playing sixteenth notes rather than eighth notes on the hi-hat adds another dimension. If you start the sixteenths with the right hand, the right hand moves to the snare drum on beats 2 and 4. If you start with the left, the left hand moves to the snare on 2 and 4. Try practicing both ways until you decide which feels best for you. In these patterns, the hands remain the same while the bass drum changes. Play them in any order.

More Advanced Sixteenth-Note Beats

In the following examples, the hands become busier while the bass drum pattern remains constant through examples 1–4 and 5–7. If you start with the left hand, all stickings are reversed.

Embellishing the Hands and Feet

More Advanced Fills

Remember to always play three bars of time before each fill. Use different time patterns, and practice this page as a complete study, moving from fill to fill in any order without stopping.

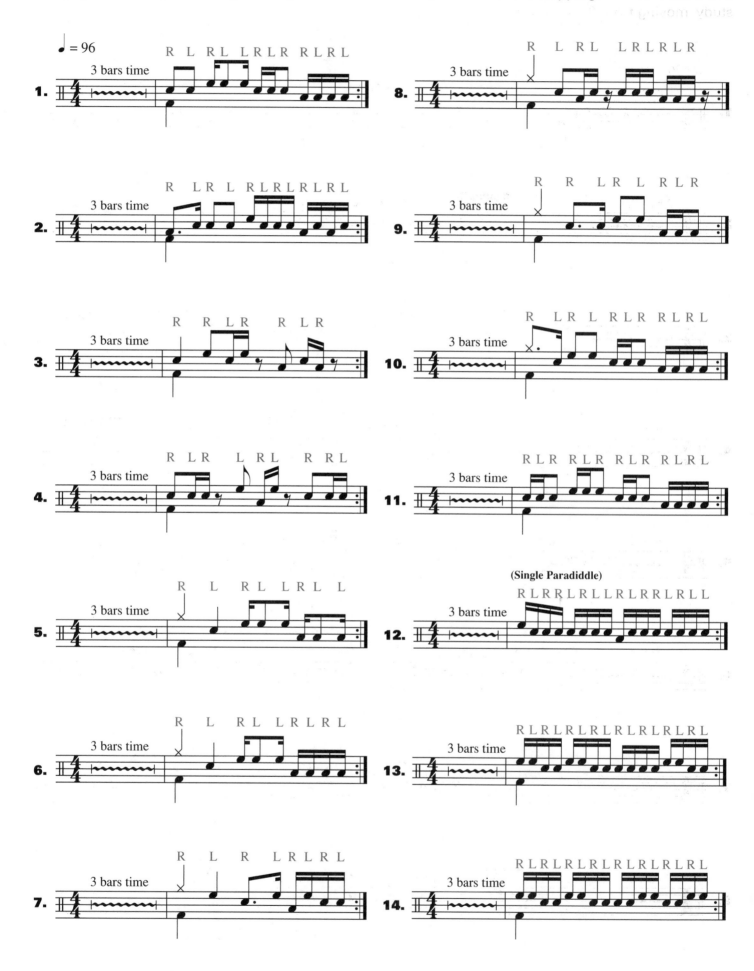

Two-Bar Fills Incorporating the Bass Drum

In this section, the bass drum is incorporated into the fill. You should play two bars of time followed by a two-bar drum fill. You may use any of the previous patterns and should play the page as a complete study, moving from fill to fill without stopping.

WINTER POEM

Winter Poem is presented twice on the DVD, first with drums, then without drums so you can play along. This chart uses some *dynamic signs* to indicate how loud or soft to play.

mp (mezzo piano) = moderately soft   ◁ (crescendo) = grow gradually louder

mf (mezzo forte) = moderately loud   ▷ (diminuendo) = grow gradually softer

BY SAMMY NESTICO
ARR. GORDON BRISKER

*See page 34.

© 1987 Fernwood Music, Inc.
Used with Permission

PLAYING JAZZ

Basic Jazz Beats

In rock, the bass drum and snare drum are of equal importance, but in jazz, the bass drum is used much less frequently, primarily just for accenting and emphasizing. The basic feel in jazz drumming comes from the cymbals, specifically the *ride rhythm* (played by the right hand on the ride cymbal) and the hi-hat (most often played on beats 2 and 4).

The ride rhythm is based on a *triplet* feel, as shown in the first example. A triplet is a group of three notes of equal value, usually played in the place of one note. Triplets have a numeral "3" placed above or beneath the center note.

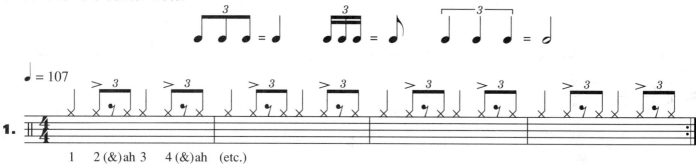

Sometimes the ride rhythm pattern is notated as follows:

Play the following basic beat in which the ride cymbal and bass drum play together. The *accent* (>) on beats 2 and 4 is crucial to the authentic jazz feel; beats 1 and 3 should be de-emphasized.

Years ago, use of the bass drum on all four beats was common practice in jazz, but it is far less common today. Practice these exercises with the bass drum on all four beats and then again with the bass drum resting. Once you're comfortable with the technique, leave the bass drum out when playing basic time.

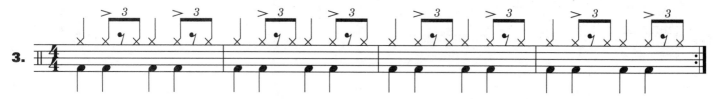

As with rock beats, the left hand (snare drum) and the left foot (hi-hat) play together as shown in the following example:

Here's a basic beat that combines both hands and both feet.

Embellishing the Left Hand

The left hand often plays eighth notes rather than quarter notes on the snare drum, as demonstrated in the following patterns. They are played with a triplet feel just as they were for the right hand. Practice these beats with the right hand first on the ride cymbal and then on the hi-hat.

Some of the notes for the left hand may be moved to a tom-tom. Example 3 adds the mounted tom-tom, example 4 adds the floor tom-tom, and examples 5 and 6 incorporate all the drums.

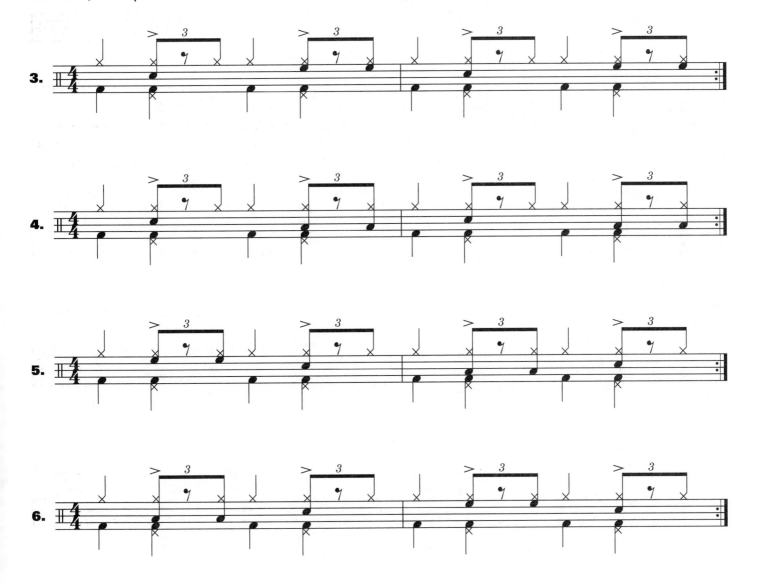

Playing on the Hi-Hat

The right hand may play the ride rhythm on the hi-hat rather than on the ride cymbal. A plus (+) sign indicates a closed hi-hat, and a small circle (○) represents an open hi-hat. When the hi-hat is in the open position, release the foot just enough so that the top cymbal slightly touches the bottom cymbal.

Like the ride cymbal, the hi-hat rhythm is based on a triplet feel, as demonstrated in the following example:

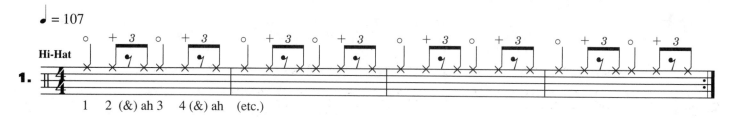

The hi-hat and bass drum play together in the following basic beat:

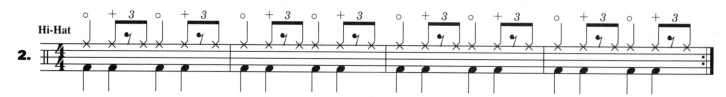

Here are some basic beats that combine both hands and both feet. Examples 4–6 are based on a two-bar pattern.

Left-Hand Independence

Left-Hand Independence Using Triplets

Jazz Fills

As in rock, jazz fills are usually played at the ends of musical phrases, serving as bridges that connect ideas. Always practice fills in a musical "time" setting, playing three bars of time followed by the fill. You may use any of the beats from the previous exercises.

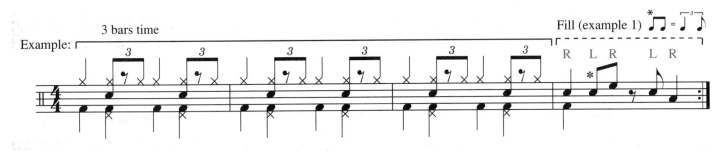

Play this page as a complete study, moving from fill to fill in any order without stopping. Remember to play three bars of time before every fill.

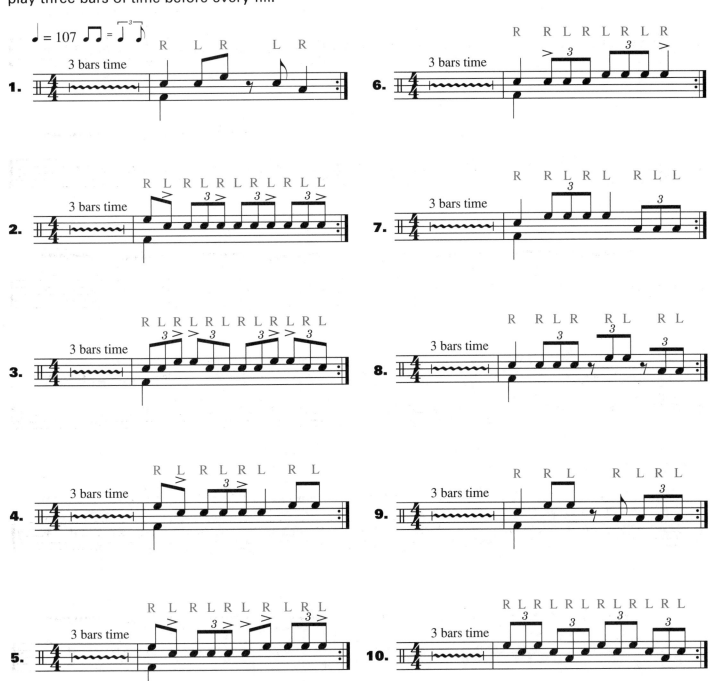

More Fills

To create an interesting variation, play the first note of each bar on the ride cymbal. This technique is demonstrated in the following patterns, but you should experiment with more of your own. Play three bars of time before each fill.

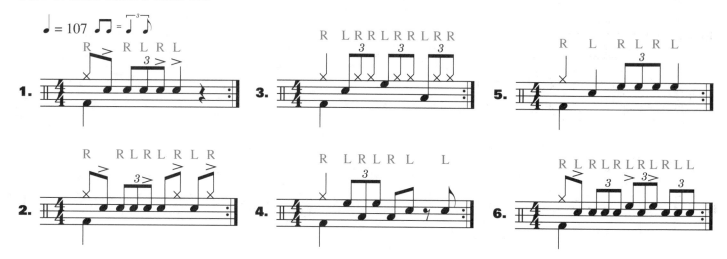

The fills in the next group are based on the same paradiddle-diddle sticking pattern learned on page 16.

Play three bars of time before each fill. Practice the examples in order horizontally across the page as well as vertically.

This pattern may also be played with a triplet feel. The first beat can be played on the snare drum or ride cymbal, and the second beat may be a note or a rest.

Two-Bar Jazz Fills

In this section, you will play two bars of time followed by a two-bar drum fill. You may use any of the beats in the previous exercises. Play this page as a complete study, moving from fill to fill in any order without stopping. Remember to play two bars of time between fills.

HAVA NICE DAY

The following tune is in **A–B–A** form, which is one of the most common ways of organizing musical thoughts. The **A** section presents the first musical idea; it is followed by a contrasting **B** section and a return to the **A** section, which may be slightly altered.

*Hava Nice Day** is presented twice on the DVD, first with drums, then without drums so you can play along.

pp (pianissimo) = very soft   *f* (forte) = loud

By Sammy Nestico
Arr. Gordon Brisker

*The big band version, as recorded by Count Basie, may be heard on the album *Hava Nice Day* (Daybreak Records, Inc.).

** = repeat the previous two bars.

Bass Drum Independence

When playing the snare drum, the left hand is often used for accents, setups and imitation. For this reason, it is not used in the following exercises devoted to basic time concepts.

Snare Drum and Bass Drum Independence

Jazz Fills Utilizing the Bass Drum

Each of these examples uses the right foot to play part of the fill. Play three bars of time before each fill using different time patterns. Practice the whole page, moving from fill to fill (with time between) in any order.

1.
2.
3.
4.
5.
6.
7.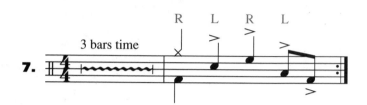
8.
9.
10.
11.
12.

More Advanced Two-Bar Fills

In this section, you will play two bars of time followed by a two-bar drum fill. You may use any of the beats from the previous exercises. Play this page as a complete study, moving from fill to fill in any order without stopping. Remember to play two bars of time between fills.

*The *drag,* also called the *3-stroke ruff,* consists of two grace notes and a main note. Play the two grace notes softer than the main note. The drag may begin with either hand.

APPENDIX

Drumhead Selection

Although drumheads were traditionally made of animal skin, today it is far more common to use heads made of synthetic material. There are numerous brands of synthetic heads on the market of varying thickness, so you must choose wisely to best fit your needs.

Tuning Your Drums

Drumheads are held in place by metal *counter-hoops* and adjusted by threaded rods. Tightening or loosening these rods alters the tension of the heads.

There are two methods for tuning drums: the *cross-tension system*, and the *clockwise system* of tensioning. The cross-tension system is the recommended method because it maintains even tensioning around the drum throughout the entire tuning process. When the clockwise system is used, however, the head tends to wrinkle in undesirable places and won't sit properly on the bearing edge, so this method of tuning is considered to be the less useful of the two. For the sake of being thorough, both methods are described below.

Cross-tension system of tensioning

As already mentioned, tuning using the cross-tension system maintains even tensioning around the drum throughout the tuning process. Tighten each screw one twist of the wrist at a time until the drumhead feels firm. Be sure not to tension any lug more than the others. Tap the head with a drumstick about two inches in from each rod to be certain the pitch is consistent around the drum. If it is not, adjust individual tension rods as needed.

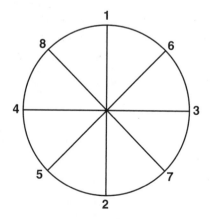

Clockwise system of tensioning

When using the clockwise system, you tune sequentially by moving in a circular fashion around the drum. Tighten each screw one twist of the wrist at a time until the drumhead feels firm. Be sure not to tension any lug more than the others. Tap the head with a drumstick about two inches in from each rod to be certain that the pitch is consistent around the drum.

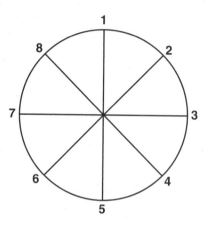

TUNING THE SNARE DRUM

The top head of a snare drum is called the *batter head*, and the bottom head is the *snare head*. It's best to start with the batter head when you tune the snare drum.

The snare head is tensioned in the same manner as the batter head. You may want to use one hand to lift the snares from the surface of the head while tensioning with the other hand to avoid snare rattle as you proceed. Tension the snare firmly, but be sure that it is still able to vibrate freely. Some drummers tighten the batter head tighter than the snare, while others do the reverse. There is no firm rule; it is simply a matter of tone preference.

Keith Moon (The Who)

Photo: Courtesy of M.C.A.

Keith Moon of The Who was one of the most influential rock drummers of all time; his often wild, expressive style reflected the general attitude of freedom and intensity that characterized the best classic rock of the 1960s and 1970s.